CONTENTS

Hawthorn High School, Hawthorn

Mali Beth Thompson (11)	1
Alexander Gadd (11)	3

Maesteg School, Maesteg

Chloe Saunders-Jones (12)	5

Milborne St Andrew First School, Milborne St Andrew

Abbie Marie White (9)	6
Ben Moody (8)	8
Rhianne O'Kelly (9)	9
Samuel Diffey (8)	10

Montem Primary School, Islington

Zoe Berhane (7)	11
Nikol Voda (9)	12
Samuel Jackson (10)	14
Ayisha Abdi (9)	15

Pakefield High School, Pakefield

Julia Stepien (11)	16
Dalton James Weatherill (11)	17
Olivia May Palmer (11)	18
Alfred James Mortlock (11)	20
Abbie Harfield (12)	21
Ryley Bell (11)	22
Jack Christopher Barker (12)	23
Imogen Wicks (12)	24
Tori Bellis (12)	25
Ciaran Howard (11)	26
Kyle Harvey Purvis (12)	27

	30
	32
...ner Richardson (12)	34
Jorja Winslade (12)	35
Keira Grubb (12)	36
Ryan Bennetts (12)	38
Lila Jones (12)	39
Jackson Roberts (12)	40
Harry Curnow (12)	42
Lily Marie Collings (12)	43
Elina Khorova (13)	44
Mea Ford (12)	45
Ella-May Matthews (12)	46
Olivia Pink (12)	48
Izzy Haughton (12)	49
Mikey Berry (12)	50
Aaron Moss (12)	51

Rice Lane Primary School, Liverpool

Callum Reece Rooney (10)	52
Mollie James (10)	54
Sophie Elizabeth Greasley (10)	55
Derry Aitken (11)	56
Jamie Tyrrell (10)	57
Sophie Bowles (10)	58
Ben Lawson (10)	59

Sacred Heart RC Primary School, South Bretton

Nicole Barton	60
Angeline Rose Caluducan (6)	61
Sithabile (Star) Mtisi	62
Adrian Kuszyk (6)	63
Tayla Nicholls (7)	64
Julia Anna Maliborska (7)	65
Joshua Antony Jose (7)	66
Sigrid Elizabeth Avenido (7)	67
Lyla Agnes Cronin (6)	68
Liliana	69
Gianluca	70
Oscar James Cornell (7)	71
Cheska Caragay	72

Shirley Community Primary School, Cambridge

Julia Reiter	73
Sophia Herriot	74
Elena Hazel Southall	75
Roberta May Rayner (9)	76
Sean Pungorn Richardson (9)	77
Shruti Saha	78
Albert	79
Joseph Owen Nathaniel Stewart (8)	80
Orrin	81
Jemima Graves	82
Edward	83

St John's College, Southsea

Ollie Lawson (11)	84
Matthew Poole (11)	86
Adam Peter Brumder (13)	88
Nuhad Zaman (12)	89
Enzo Richardson (12)	90
Grace Hooper (12)	91
Sophia Baxter (12)	92
Elyza Jan Parazo (14)	93
Finley George Steele (11)	94

St Patrick's Primary School, Eskra

Christy Meegan (10)	95
Berneen Gilroy (10)	96

The County High School, Leftwich

Phoebe Ryle (13)	97

The Wigston Academies Trust, Wigston

Lucy Tunnicliffe (12)	98
Woody Orton (12)	100

Wetherby Senior School, London

Alexandre Nasser (11)	101
Oscar Jaworski (11)	102
Billy Carter (11)	105
Elijah Newman (11)	107

Willingham Primary School, Willingham

Alistair Rountree (10)	110
Jenny May Slater (9)	112
Nia Lily Rose Mills (9)	113
Isla Hayes (9)	114

Woodside High School, Wood Green

Hang Tran (13)	115
Charles William Laurence (13)	116
Charlie Pablo (14)	118
Sophia Andi Neofetou (14)	120
Elena Rosetta Di Natale (14)	121

Awesome Creations

Edited By Jenni Harrison

First published in Great Britain in 2020 by:

Young Writers
Remus House
Coltsfoot Drive
Peterborough
PE2 9BF
Telephone: 01733 890066
Website: www.youngwriters.co.uk

All Rights Reserved
Book Design by Ashley Janson
© Copyright Contributors 2020
Softback ISBN 978-1-83928-580-6

Printed and bound in the UK by BookPrintingUK
Website: www.bookprintinguk.com
YB0434H

FOREWORD

Young Writers was established in 1991 to promote poetry and nurture the creative writing talent in school children across the UK and overseas. Today we continue to provide a platform for children and young adults to showcase their work. Our latest competition, Phizz-Whizzing Words, was created to celebrate Roald Dahl Day on 13th September.

One of the world's most beloved children's authors, Roald Dahl has delighted readers, young and old, with his unique and fantastical stories for over 50 years. To join in the celebrations on Roald Dahl Day, we invited young authors to pen a story or poem of their own.

Taking inspiration from Roald Dahl's interesting and loveable characters, use of language and exciting plot lines, these young writers have shown their creative writing skills by creating their own imaginative and inventive tales and poems. With crazy creatures, mysterious happenings and cruel guardians getting their comeuppance, this is a collection that will delight readers of any age.

The Creative Writing

Matilda

The story starts with Matilda and the marvellous Miss Honey, enjoying their tea when a lightning storm struck the house. The house set on fire. They had to live on the street. When Matilda thought nothing could get any worse, it did. Matilda's parents came and demanded Matilda come home. Miss Honey gave up on Matilda and allowed her to leave with her parents. Matilda went home and watched the horrid Miss Trunchbull and Miss Honey. Miss Honey was carrying a shrink-ray gun.

They took Matilda to the school and Miss Honey shrank the school. They warned her that that would happen to her and everyone she loved unless she gave back the old doll she stole from Miss Trunchbull's that day, Matilda hadn't realised its value.

So she spent most of her day thinking of a way to stop Miss Honey and Miss Trunchbull. Then she realised that Charlie was at the factory and could help. Matilda explained everything and so they set up a trap involving whizz-popping chocolate. It would catch them in a net so they could grab the shrink-ray gun.

They led Miss Honey and Miss Trunchbull by leaving a chocolate cake so they would go and get the cake and it worked. They grasped at the spectacular gun and unshrank the school. Matilda asked Miss Trunchbull

why she wanted it and she said the doll was valuable and worth £6 million pounds. Miss Trunchbull went to jail and they all celebrated.

Mali Beth Thompson (11)
Hawthorn High School, Hawthorn

The Enormous Crocodile's Revenge

The enormous jaws snapped shut, grabbing a bright shining star and gobbling it up with greed. His tail still hurt from where the elephant's great, mighty trunk had crushed it, and he felt dizzy from where the harrowing elephant had spun him round like a whizzy didgeridoo. But now, the enormous crocodile was plummeting to Earth, his bright green scales shimmering in the rising sun. He wanted to destroy that elephant and he knew just who to ask for help.

Splash! He hit the sea with a deafening crash, his body aching as he crawled on to land. Basking in the sunlight, a toothy grin crept across his face as five enormous shadows eclipsed the sun, stealing his warmth. Five colossal giants towered over him, excited as he explained his plan. Giants loved eating children, so if he lured them here, the elephant was sure to follow.

The giants quickly rushed to Petty-Monshay and bought a stupendous sandwich as big as twenty sofas and put up a sign that read: *Free Wi-Fi.*

That night, as planned, the children came and while distracted, playing on their mobile phones, the crocodile climbed into the sandwich to hide. Suddenly, the sandwich closed, trapping him and the children inside. The giants took a bite and immediately started to swell up. They were allergic to crocodile scales.

Pop! The giants exploded and all that could be seen, illuminated by the lights of the children's mobile phones was a big sticky mess and the silhouette of a ghastly, harrowing elephant.

Alexander Gadd (11)
Hawthorn High School, Hawthorn

Roald Dahl

R oald Dahl has written lots of amazing books
O ld, new and funny ones too
A ll the books are good to read
L ove reading? Me too so
D on't stop reading these page-turners.

D o you have fun reading?
A book is a great escape, especially my favourite, 'Charlie and the Chocolate Factory'
H ave fun reading the adventure and exploring with Roald Dahl
L et's keep reading and let's see what comes next.

Chloe Saunders-Jones (12)
Maesteg School, Maesteg

Hermione Kindly

Be prepared to read about Hermione Kindly and Mr and Mrs Kindly and Lily Bulitons. It all started when Hermione was walking to school. Okay, nothing unusual there. Anyway, let's skip that bit. She got to school and was having break but unlike any other year seven she wasn't into texting, doing make-up or anything like that. She was a girl who liked to read. She would always sit by a tree. Her favourite books were Linda Chapmen.

But one break, she saw a girl covered in cuts and bruises. Hermione decided to go over. So that's what she did.

She went over and asked for her name but before she could finish, the girl snapped, "Don't even think of making fun of me."

But instead of getting angry, she said calmly, "I'm trying to help. What's your name?"

"Li-Lily," she muttered. "Lily Buliton."

Hermione sat beside her.

"How old are you?" she asked.

"Eight," said Lily.

Hermione helped the girl up.

"Why aren't you in there with the others?"

The girl didn't answer.

"Can I come to your house?"

"Yes," Hermione said.
The end of school came and they walked together. Hermione's parents greeted her. They went to Hermione's room.
Soon, Lily trusted her and said, "My parents want to get rid of me."
Hermione jumped up and said, "My parents will adopt you."
Hermione's parents said yes and soon adopted her. And she had a much better life with her new sister and new parents.

Abbie Marie White (9)
Milborne St Andrew First School, Milborne St Andrew

Amazon Adventure

Once, in a small cottage, there lived a happy family that owned a farm. All day they worked, all day long. One day, George wanted to see the rainforest so he booked a flight to the rainforest, the Amazon rainforest. So the next morning, he said goodbye to his family and set off on his adventure to the Amazon. On the way, he watched TV and played on his tablet too and then he was there. In the Amazon, he went to his hotel where he would stay for the night. The next morning, he would get up and explore the rainforest and its myths and stay for two days, then go home. The next morning, he woke up and went to the rainforest. He walked through the dense undergrowth until he came across an old, little, wooden tree house and saw a boy and he was a nine-year-old boy. He was getting water from a well then he went inside and George followed and the boy turned.
"My name is Squareyes."
"Hello, Squareyes, my name is George," he said.
Then he said, "Do you like pineapple juice?"
"Yes," said George.
"Then have some of my pineapple juice."
So he had some and went off again with Squareyes and he said, "I know where a watering hole is."
So he went and had fun and together they got on the plane back home.

Ben Moody (8)
Milborne St Andrew First School, Milborne St Andrew

Horatio Lullaby

First, I'll introduce you to Horatio Lullaby, she is a rather bossy child. She is also annoying, posh, nosy, unhealthy and loves to sing. The food she loves the most is toad-in-the-hole. Let's make it sound a little... okay, a lot less gross, it's basically sausages in pancake mix.

Now let me introduce you to the bully, Nicolas Nasey. Ten years ago, Nicolas snuck home from school to make a forget-everything gadget. The next day, he zapped the teacher and had a party! Such a naughty boy. Another thing about Nicolas is that he is a bouncing whatsit which means someone who can't sit still.

Oh, I nearly forgot, Horatio has a pet called Bolt. He is the key here because he always gets into a battle-tattle. I think that you know what that means! So as I was saying about the bully, they say he mustn't be tricked. Be aware of what happens next...

Nicolas tried to use the forget-everything gadget on Horatio because he was jealous. But Bolt came to the rescue and turned Nicolas Nasey into a Rhinostossteriss with one quick wag of his tail. You should have seen poor Nicolas, he was petrified! Horatio now became the favourite, top of the school and Nick was only able to say rubbsquash for the rest of his sorry, little Rhinostossteriss life!

Rhianne O'Kelly (9)
Milborne St Andrew First School, Milborne St Andrew

Horatio Honeybee

Once upon a time, there lived a girl named Horatio Honeybee. Her favourite author by far was Roald Dahl. She wanted to make a surprise party for him so she did. She came out to a large field and got to work cutting it. Five hours later, it was cut and Horatio's hands were aching.

The next day, she got to work on the stalls and the prize stand for the golden book cover! Now she had to get all of the food ready like the chicken, pizza and cheeseburgers. The best thing was that the party did not cost a thing because everything was made. Then she made the invitations and it took hours.

By the time she had finished, she realised there was an eagle next filled with eggs but the mum and dad were nowhere to be seen. So she clipped half of the tree so you could see it. Then she covered it in yellow and black tape. It was an oak tree so it was hard because every time the eggs wobbled, acorns fell on her head and kept knocking her down.

The next day, everyone came and had loads of fun. There were loads of Roald Dahl books, posters, plushies and figures.

As everyone started to leave, a boy screamed, "The eggs are hatching!"

Because the eagle mum and dad were gone, everyone got to take one of the cute babies.

Samuel Diffey (8)

Milborne St Andrew First School, Milborne St Andrew

Silly Wonker And The Chocolate Factory

Willy Wonka decided to go on holiday and left his brother Silly Wonker in charge of his factory. Silly Wonker had a habit of making silly mistakes but this time he was determined to be responsible. After walking around and taking a tour, Silly Wonker became quite bored so he tried to make a new invention. He tried to invent a new type of chocolate but everything went wrong. He mixed bubblegum and chocolate and it turned into chocolate super glue! It grew really big and stuck all the Oompa-Loompas to the wall! He then tried something else! He mixed ice cream and candyfloss hoping for some great new flavours but it turned into freezing fur balls that shed hair everywhere like a cat. "I can't clean this all before Willy Wonka comes back!" He tried to pull the Oompa-Loompas off the wall but it was too hard. So then he had a crazy idea! He started to eat away at the chocolate super glue and finally, the Oompa-Loompas started to come down. They helped Silly Wonker to clean the factory all up. Just as they finished, they heard a key turn in the gate.
"It must be Willy Wonka!" whispered Silly Wonker.
The door opened, and there he stood with a big smile on his face as the factory looked exactly the same as how he left it. Willy Wonka never found out about the mess.

Zoe Berhane (7)
Montem Primary School, Islington

The Love Of Stories

It was late into the night, when the phone started to ring. It was midnight and I had a feeling that it was going to be some bad news. Without hesitating, I opened the door of my room and ran across the hall, down the stairs in the dark.

"Dad, what's going on? Is everything okay?"

I saw him standing quietly in front of the viewless window looking sad.

"Go to bed son, it's late, we'll speak tomorrow morning," he said.

I couldn't sleep all night, I felt something was wrong. Mum came into my room first thing in the morning looking very worried and told me to get ready to go to the hospital because granny was extremely ill.

"Hi Granny Nila, I've missed you!"

"I've missed you too! Read me some stories! I need something to keep me alive here!"

I started to read Granny some of my favourite Roald Dahl stories. I started with Matilda. She loved how brave and sweet she was and got excited when the wicked Miss Trunchball got defeated and clapped her hands. Then I read her 'The BFG' - she was amazed at how giant he was! Finally, 'Charlie and Chocolate Factory' - she loved the adventure and it even made her hungry for some delicious chocolate. Suddenly,

Granny was propped up on her bed with lots of energy and a huge appetite! It was at that moment that everyone realised, Granny wasn't sick at all, she had just been bored!

Nikol Voda (9)
Montem Primary School, Islington

Roald Dahl World

As I walked through the busy streets of London trying not to lose hope, I reflected on my life. I thought about my cruel and horrendous parents. They were a very mean couple and only cared about playing games. They thought I was sinful and embarrassing just for wanting to read and learn. When they thought they'd had enough of my desire for knowledge, they abandoned me. If I'm honest, I didn't want to live with them anyway!

A few days later, I was sat in my usual corner, shivering and hungry. A man approached me and made an offer. He introduced himself as 'Roald Dahl'.

"Do you want to join a magical world?"

I had nothing to lose, so I accepted and that's where the adventure began. He took me up into a glass lift and to an enormous chocolate factory. I gazed in amazement! Then I entered a huge dream-world that had a storage of 150,000,225 dreams! Then, finally, he took me to a place that he called special and told me that I could call it home. It was in a mansion that used to be owned by Miss Trunchbull.

"Here you can learn and read as much as you want! Miss Honey and Matilda will look after you very well."

Samuel Jackson (10)
Montem Primary School, Islington

The Amazing Roald Dahl

The Twits was a horrid story,
It was bad for children, way too gory!
The Witches made me tremble hard,
Whilst Charlie had fun in a chocolate cart!
Matilda's parents never loved her,
Plus, she was bullied by her brother.
Mr Twit's beard was a mess.
It was as frilly as Veruca's dress
But all of this doesn't matter.
Roald Dahl is crazier than the mad hatter!
He can make you smile or snarl.
So let us welcome the amazing Roald Dahl!

Ayisha Abdi (9)
Montem Primary School, Islington

Untitled

The end... yes, I know most stories don't start like that but this story is unique, so my life is quite... backwards. My name is Xela and my second name is, well... Alex, and if you didn't realise, Xela is Alex backwards. It's weird but I love my life... kinda.

It all started at college when it all went wrong, I was all alone and I didn't really know anyone anymore. I didn't even know the way around the school, which meant I had to talk to someone. So I walked up to an elephant, also known as the school bully. He was a huge guy with monkey hair and elephant arms and yes, you guessed it, he would bully me every day and call me Alex. He would say I'm a boy, even though I'm a girl. But it wouldn't stop me from working hard at... getting a friend and up to today, I was so lonely.

Once, I met a boy, his name was Zach and no, no, no, this isn't turning into a love story because that's ewwww! He turned into my friend. He was such a cronkyzip which means he was a crazy monkey. We would hang out 24/7. He would call me a dog, so I called him a monkey as he was a cronkyzip. We would always help each other if we were upset.

Julia Stepien (11)
Pakefield High School, Pakefield

Bullying

On a sunny day in the tree family, Aarava was sleeping. Stone-heartedly, her dad stormed into the room and shouted, "You meddling bophanger! Wake up!"
Aarava sighed and climbed down her bunk bed which was for her sister before she passed away. She went downstairs and saw her cereal out. She was given very little cereal while her brother had mountains of it. After finishing her cereal in a record of three seconds, she stomped upstairs and got dressed. Her flushbuckling dad ignored her while she got on her bus. When she got to school, Trunchbull Jr, a heartless bully, grabbed her collar against a locker and slapped her.
"You didn't do my homework, you slurry hare-brained dog!"
She had finally had enough and hit her so hard she spat out blood in defeat.
"Never touch me again!"
Aarava limped away happily.

Dalton James Weatherill (11)
Pakefield High School, Pakefield

Teachers

Teachers are cruel,
Teachers are evil,
Teachers are the worst living people alive,
"Do your homework or detention!"
Revolting little creatures take over our lives,
Run! Run! Teachers are coming
If they find you, detention is all yours.

Ugly people take over our childhood,
Smelly old witches are the worst teachers in the world,
Putting tricks and spells on us to make them laugh,
Everybody is moody in class,
Nothing to do,
Nothing to say,
All we do is sit down, all down, all day,
Boys want to go home and play on their video games,
While girls want to take pictures and go shopping for the rest of the day.

The end of the day,
It's the best part of the day,
The teacher and the class walking outside to the parents,
And at the end of the day,
After your teacher has been cruel,

She acts all kind to you and gives you a high-five and says,
"Well done today, you were amazing!"
But she isn't nice for long.

Olivia May Palmer (11)
Pakefield High School, Pakefield

Goblins!

The story begins in a small town called Scurvy Shrimps, a seaside town north of Lowestoft. The people are friendly and they have record-breaking fish and chips. The town is really a fishing town.

One fateful day, a meteor the size of a small town came crashing down at the speed of light. When it hit, the people went to investigate. A goblin horde spilt out and attacked people, they pillaged the houses and ate all the food. The townspeople had nothing to do.

A few days passed, the people were all tired so they went to the king and explained the goblin problem. The king was surprised but he sent soldiers to kill the goblins, the people were happy. The soldiers confronted the goblins but they trembled with fear and ran with fear, except for one soldier, just a boy who stood his ground...

Alfred James Mortlock (11)
Pakefield High School, Pakefield

Madalyn Mon Creek

"Tonight, in the moonlight, I shall seek all the monsters that lurk beneath!" exclaimed Madalyn Mon Creek.
It all started when the nice Madalyn Mon Creek was on her way to the family vacation in the dark, gloomy house on the hill. She stepped out of her car and she looked up, the house had vamprats on the roof. She screamed and shouted as loud as she could. Madalyn ran into the house, slammed the door and hid in the cupboard for several days.
Ten days later, she came out; dark, scary Madalyn Mon Creek. While she was in the cupboard, she had hatched an evil plan to bring back the dead, vampires, werewolves and all the gothcats that had been dead for thousands of years. She got mongle weed, and all the ingredients she needed to do the spell...

Abbie Harfield (12)
Pakefield High School, Pakefield

The Twins

These twins were called Jimmy and Jimbo, they both despised each other. They were both eleven years old. One day at high school, Jimmy asked for help in maths. Jimbo called Jimmy across the room.
"You decayed, lily-livered popinjay!"
Then Jimmy replied, "You revolting, mad wag."
Then the day ended. The bus picked them up, but the driver didn't like children. He took the job then kidnapped a kid every day. It was one of the twins' turn! They kept forcing each other to go first. Little did they know that whatever kid went first didn't get off ever, ever again! Soon after that day, Jimmy never got the bus again. Was it just karma?

Ryley Bell (11)
Pakefield High School, Pakefield

The Haunted House

In the dark, gloomy house, in the middle of the forest, the family of four and their dogs were killed outside the gates in a car crash. The mum, dad, brother and dogs were content to walk the hallways but the sister was always wanting to frighten people.

In the village, a boy called Joe lived with his friends. One day, Joe and his friend went to the dark, gloomy house.

They walked up the path, looked at each other and said, "Fiddlesticks."

They opened the front door, the sister ghost jumped out, then the sister ghost dragged them upstairs and they were never seen again.

Jack Christopher Barker (12)
Pakefield High School, Pakefield

Roald Dahl

R oald Dahl, children's author
O riginal tales
A lways wrote in pencil on yellow paper
L oved chocolate but not chocolate cake or chocolate ice cream
D ictionary at hand.

D ied on the 23rd of November 1990
A nnounced dinner was ready by saying, "Nose bags on," or "Grubs up!"
H ard work all day
L aughter of children for generations.

Imogen Wicks (12)
Pakefield High School, Pakefield

Terror Awaits

Walking through the graveyard gates,
Here is where the terror awaits!
Lurking in the fog and mist,
Was something that hissed
All I wanted to do was take a stroll through the park,
I didn't know something would be hiding in the dark,
Petrified, I let out a scream,
Was this some kind of dream?
A large pack of werewolves jumped out at me
And moved closer,
Bizzfizz!
Grumblewink!

Tori Bellis (12)
Pakefield High School, Pakefield

The Wicked Headteacher

Once upon a time, not that long ago
There was a school called Madwageo
In this school, there was a wicked headteacher
His head was no longer there
This is for the woeful and whimpering and
Children with powers like disappearing and killing
The people pass by managing to kill
The woeful master, also known as
Headteacher Twittler
Nobody wins... ever
All die, never to be seen again.

Ciaran Howard (11)
Pakefield High School, Pakefield

Night Fight

In the middle of the night, I went for a walk to the park. I saw a big monster in the park with a knife! The monster was looking at me, I was shaken then there were zombies coming out from nowhere.
I was terrified and let out a scream. I wish it was a terrible dream. They went to break my neck and I kicked the zombie in the head then he hit the deck. That silly Fizzlecump should not have messed with me.

Kyle Harvey Purvis (12)
Pakefield High School, Pakefield

Horror Night

Walking through the graveyard gate,
A night of terrifying horror awaits,
The gate slams shut behind me,
I feel like I'll never be free,
As the mist rolls along the yard,
I am going to find this really hard,
Then I realise a shadow flies past,
I don't think I'll ever last.

Ruby Sims (12)
Pakefield High School, Pakefield

The Story Of Johny

Johny, a thirteen-year-old boy, had been sat watching TV when an ageing man walked in with Johny's mother. They sat and said, "Johny, you have a very special power, you can shape-shift."

Johny could hardly believe it.

He thought it was some sort of joke but eventually when he stopped laughing, he looked at his mum and said, "Are you being serious?"

She just stared at him, so Johny got up and thought, *I want to be a dragon*, but unsurprisingly, it didn't work. His mum told him he needed to feel the right emotions but he kept asking his mum questions like, "So why hasn't it happened yet?" or, "If I do have powers, why didn't you tell me earlier?"

The next morning, Johny got up, but he didn't feel right and it wasn't because he was tired, so he went to the bathroom and saw he was a sloth. He thought to himself, *it worked! Maybe feelings affect it as well*. By the time he walked back to his room, he was human again. He got changed and went downstairs to get breakfast. On the way to the kitchen, he stubbed his toe. Because he was angry, he turned into a bull. He now knew that whatever happened to him and the way he felt, meant that he turned into different animals. From now on, he learnt to control his emotions because of fear of turning into an animal in front of people. To this day, he still turns into animals so keep a look out for him.

Logan Macnab (12)
Penrice Academy, St Austell

The Mysterious Bed

Boing! Boing! Fin went bouncing up and down. *Boing!* Fin Wilder was an energetic child. He had sky-blue eyes, gleaming white teeth, pale skin and messy brown hair.
"Fin, stop bouncing on your bed or it will break!" shouted Fin's mum.
"I'll be fi- " Fin yelled as his bed suddenly collapsed below him. "Erm, Mum, you know you said my bed would break?"
Later that day, in Cheepo Furniture, Fin and his mum went looking for a new bed. Most beds were lots of money but after what felt like days of shopping, they finally found a bed. The bed was small with a creature on each bedpost, Fin wasn't sure on the bed but, as soon as his mum saw it was £5, he knew what was going to happen.
Soon after, they were driving home with the bed attached to the roof of the car. After lunch, Fin was kicking a football around his room when the ball went flying under his bed. Reluctantly, he went and crawled under to get it. Suddenly, Fin was in a different world with mountains and snow and there was his ball at the bottom. Slowly, Fin shuffled over the edge and slipped! Quickly, he rolled down the mountain and collapsed. He opened his eyes and above him was a yeti. Fin looked at the yeti, the yeti looked back, then at the football. Little did Fin know that he had found the only

footballing yeti. Quickly, the yeti kicked the ball up the hill and slowly, Fin trudged up thinking about what had happened.

Sam Hoffen (12)
Penrice Academy, St Austell

The Worst Dream

"Where's my money?" shouted Veronica as she chased a ten-year-old down the street.
The only sound to be heard was them. They turned a corner and the ten-year-old was gone. Veronica turned around and headed for her grandad's house. Every week she got advice from him. He was nice to her and friendly, unlike her family who she thought didn't even know she existed.
A couple of weeks later, her grandad died. Everyone was sad, but nothing could compare to the sorrow Veronica felt. That day she bullied more than ever just to get her sadness out. Nothing worked, she was still sad.
That night, she packed her clothes and left. She ran as fast as she could out of her village and into the woods. It was dark, pitch-black as she fell asleep under a tree. She heard rustling in the bushes next to her. She thought nothing of it.
In the morning, she woke to a roar nearby. She stood up and waited. The next roar was even closer. She started running but didn't know where to go. soon, she ran into a corner and was face-to-face with a bear. The giant mouth lunged towards her and...
Sweat was running down her head like a waterfall, as she opened her eyes, she was in her room.

"What happened?" She ran downstairs to find her family making breakfast.
"You okay darling? You look like you've been eaten by a bear!"

Holly Crompton (12)
Penrice Academy, St Austell

The Jungle Girl

"I'm leaving! I can't do this anymore!"
Alice Page ran down the dusty road, carrying her toothbrush in one hand and a hairband in the other. It had been four years since the terrible fallout she had with her horrid parents. Now, she was sat watching the monkeys hang from tree to tree and the parrots dancing in the sky. She lay silently on her leaf bed. Suddenly, the sound of metal hit the rocks in the lake. Alice found a small bottle floating around, she slowly opened it to find a letter reading: 'Dear Alice, it's me, Rose, your sister. I need your help. Mum and Dad are being so, so mean. I've started sailing to your jungle, we need to get revenge. Yours sincerely, Rose'.

As Alice began to read the letter, she thought to herself, *is it time? Is it time to use my jungle powers on them?* Three hours later, the girls and all the animals hopped onto the boat and began their journey back to get revenge. All the birds set up the sail.

Slowly, the door creaked open as the girls entered the house. They rushed around trying to find their parents. "Oi you, both of you get lost. We were happy without you!" screamed their parents.

At a halt, Alice did her jungle spell on them.

Two years later... their parents had had the tragedy of being bears and slaves for their children!

Summer Richardson (12)
Penrice Academy, St Austell

My Story

As Pheebee was just getting out of bed, she realised that news reporters were surrounding her so she pushed all of them out the way but funnily enough, her twin brother, James, who is a normal teenage, grumpy boy, had the exact same room, just different colours. Then James came running out of his room, telling Pheebee everything, that he had the same powers as her and that their stepmum knew all about their secret and that they should run away and find somewhere to live so no one could keep them as hostages.

"We can go live on the houseboat, there are beds and food there. Both of us need to pack the essentials like money and other stuff, keep it small."

Finally, James was ready. About half an hour later, they settled on the houseboat, sailing across the river, it was so peaceful. Two weeks later, their stepmum found them and put them in captivity.

She said, "You can't walk out that door."

Then James and Pheebee broke out of the rope they were tied to and said, "We don't need to walk, we can fly!"

So they flew out the door like there was no tomorrow. They flew to Cornwall, England and lived with their grandparents and their real mum.

Jorja Winslade (12)
Penrice Academy, St Austell

My Story

Harriet's curly, long, blonde hair bounced up and down as she skipped across the pavement. Her pink dress swayed in the wind with her pink shoes tapping against the cold, hard concrete. Nobody would guess that a perfect girl was secretly plotting evil ways to torture her brother.
She thought back to yesterday when she pulled clingfilm over the door. Poor Joshua fell for it and smashed his head on the cold wooden floor.
Suddenly, because she was so deep in thought, she walked straight into the door of her house! She was knocked out. It was 5pm when her parents found her. Two hours. Five hours. Ten hours. Twelve hours later, she woke up in a hospital, strapped to the pristine white bed. Suddenly, she got a temptation to scream.
"I'm sorry!" she suddenly wailed. "I pulled all those horrible pranks on Joshua, I thought it was funny at the time, which it was, but now I just feel like the worst sister in the world!"
Her parents just stood there, over the hospital bed. Shocked. Then her father unstrapped her from the bed and pulled her up and took her home.
"Pack your bags!" he sang. "We are moving to America!"

After that, nobody ever saw the Hector family again and Harriet lived a great American life with her pink shoes tapping against the cold, hard concrete...

Keira Grubb (12)
Penrice Academy, St Austell

Body Chronicles

Timmy the Toenail is a young, growing toenail. His dad, Fred the Foot, loves him so much but his mum, Lila the Leg, prefers his sister, Abby the Arm.

It was just an ordinary day when out of the blue, a lovely woman came out from behind the tree, it was Naomi the Neck. Timmy had had a crush on her for ages. Someone else came out from behind the tree, it was Harley the Head. Naomi had told him she had a boyfriend but he thought she was playing hard to get. He remembered when they first met, his cheeks were puffy and red as he stood and watched at a distance and then reality kicked in, he got rejected.

Timmy the Toenail ran as fast and as far as he could until he met someone he didn't know so he was cautious.

"I will call the police, I'm not scared. Oh wait, I've got no fingers."

And the stranger said, "Hi Timmy, I'm your uncle, Eden the Eye."

Uncle Eden approached him but Timmy was still cautious but let him approach him and then out of nowhere, Eden's friends came out of nowhere but Timmy scratched them all and blinded them. Timmy ran home and spread the news. His mum, Lila the Leg, appreciated him more now.

Ryan Bennetts (12)
Penrice Academy, St Austell

Billie Stocking

Billie was a very mistreated child, who had been pushed way too far and was now out for revenge. The young girl was born on September 1st along with her perfect twin sister, Kate. Mr and Mrs Stocking had always favoured Kate, ever since the day she was born and now at the age of eleven, Billie had had enough... It was Monday 21st January and it was the first day of school for both the twins. No, they didn't go to the same school. Kate went to an amazing private school in the centre of London and Billie just went to a rubbish school around the corner from they lived. Billie wasn't too bothered as long as she went to school and wasn't stuck with her horrible parents she was the happiest girl alive. That evening, Billie arrived home, buzzing with excitement as she had heard there were some spots open for an exquisite theatre nearby. She skipped over to her mother and asked to audition! She said no. Billie then asked Father. He said no. Tears dripped down the poor girl's rosy cheeks as she ran into her bedroom, slamming the door behind her. While sitting on the floor, Billie spotted a book, a book about how to get revenge on your parents...

Lila Jones (12)
Penrice Academy, St Austell

Captain Obvious

Captain Obvious was obviously an obvious person,
He always wore a shirt that said 'obvious' on it,
As well as a sailor's hat so everyone knew he was a captain,
Obviously, an obvious fit for Captain Obvious.

People would sigh and shout when he walked down the street,
"Ugh, it's Captain Obvious again."
And obviously Captain Obvious would reply,
"Who else would I be? Someone's Great-Uncle Ben?"
Truly the most obvious thing to say.

He would work at his office job,
Blurting obvious things along the way,
Sliding his chair side to side,
The only way a chair should sway.

He always goes to the shop on his way home,
Getting an obvious amount of fruits and veggies,
He'd grab his dinner, dessert and other delectable delicacies,
And walk back to what was obviously his home.

Later, as Captain Obvious got in his house,
He sat down on his bed to lay,
There was one obvious question at the end of the day,
Why did I write this poem this way?

Jackson Roberts (12)
Penrice Academy, St Austell

Story

I am running down the path, through the forest after this strange creature with dark fur and blue eyes jumped out of a bush and started chasing me. So I'm going to my hideout.

It all started two hours ago when I took my first step into the forest to collect some apples for my lunch. Everything was fine until there was some rattling coming from the bush, and it was at that moment when I realised that I should run.

I am now in my hideout and the creature has broken in. I run to the shed, pick up a shovel and hide behind the door.

"Where are you? I know my lunch is somewhere in he-..."

I whack him square in the face and he is now knocked out on the floor.

"Looks like you're gonna be my dinner now!"

I am now going home to celebrate my victory with family and friends and cook our dinner. Today is a special meal that we have never had before, so we need to make sure that it is cooked to perfection for us all to enjoy.

Harry Curnow (12)
Penrice Academy, St Austell

My Roald Dahl Poem

Poor Abby was only four years old
And her scary dad was big and bald
Her little brother whose name was Greg
His favourite food was scrambled egg
Her evil mum whose name was Gregina,
And I know what you're thinking, she was a lot meaner.

All Abby liked to do was scream and play,
So she would be out with her friends all day!
But little Abby was not very fair,
She pushed her best friend off her chair.

She was thinking all day about running away,
So she packed her bags for a one night stay!
She ran away but not very far
Until she noticed a familiar car.

She had thought, *oh no, they're gonna take me back*
So she hid inside a dusty old potato sack!

Six months later and I know you want to hear the rest
Who would have thought she had turned out to be the best?

Lily Marie Collings (12)
Penrice Academy, St Austell

Violet

Violet is a girl with charcoal-black hair and ocean-blue eyes,
She lives with her father in the grand house,
One day, she saw as the sky lies,
A wrecked boat and a tiny doghouse,
"How did the boat come here?" questioned Violet
Then she went to the forest,
She saw an aeroplane with a pilot,
Then a man appeared asking, "Are you a florist?"

She was shocked in horror, nearly drawing a gun out of her coat,
But then she turned around and realised, he was a ghost,
He looked like he was from a story that her friend wrote,
Then he tried to explain to me that he's from a coast,
But that's when she noticed it was twelve o'clock,
She ran like she never ran before,
She went into her house and heard a knock,
And it was the ghost once more.

Elina Khorova (13)
Penrice Academy, St Austell

Trapped Boy

There was a girl called Scarlet aged eight,
She lived in the jungle with her mate,
As they were walking through the trees,
The air was warm as there was no breeze,
As dawn struck, the friends awoke,
And what they found make them stoked,
"Our bear trap worked!" they exclaimed with joy
But not a bear, it had caught a boy!
"Arghhhh! Help!" he screamed with all his might,
The girls did not expect that fright,
They found some rope and climbed the tree,
The boy's face brightened with glee,
He said, "You saved my life you amazing girls, you..."
But before he finished, he fell in some poo!
Before the girls had time to giggle,
They helped the boy out of his pickle.

Mea Ford (12)
Penrice Academy, St Austell

The Cheese, The Rat And The Cat

The cheese sat there,
Staring at the stair,
With its golden glow,
Looking like snow,
The holes were deep,
Enough to put you asleep,
The long corridors,
And wooden floors,
Were dull,
And it smelt like coal,
Through the cracks of the walls,
A fat little rat calls,
"Get me some cheese or I won't say, please!"
Quietly, the cat lay
Watching out for its prey,
"Come here rat, I will squish you flat."
The rat scurries to the cheese,
Begging on his knees,
That he'll make it,
But there was a problem,
He was inside the cheese,
"Oh golly gumdrops,
This is the end of me,

I think I need a pee,
Oh no, he's coming for me."

Ella-May Matthews (12)
Penrice Academy, St Austell

The Rat In The Hat

The rat in the hat,
Except the rat wasn't in the hat,
The hat was sat on the living room floor,
Mr Rat came and sat on my lap,
Mr Rat wanted more,
He was too ratty,
He wanted to look a bit more tatty,
So he popped off to the shop,
He bought a lot of tatty clothes,
He hitched a ride and drove back home,
When he got home, he tucked into his hat,
But he wanted to sit on my lap instead,
He looked a bit tatty,
He was too obviously tatty and wanted ratty back,
This was the rat in the hat,
But here's the catch,
He is a human,
The rat wasn't a rat,
The hat wasn't a hat,
There wasn't a rat in a hat any longer.

Olivia Pink (12)
Penrice Academy, St Austell

One Of A Kind

Splash! Crash!
Splish! Splosh!
Here she comes with her amazing trot,
Out of the sea, straight at me.

Tail wags from side to side,
In the sand she does hide,
She rolls around all of the day,
Oh, how she loves to always play.

Her bark can sometimes drive me mad,
Her bites and scratches sometimes make me sad,
But her smile for me is always there,
With loyalty, love and lots of care.

Izzy Haughton (12)
Penrice Academy, St Austell

Twilight

Joe Underwood is just a boy,
A boy with an imagination,
This imagination is something to behold.

Joe Underwood is just a boy,
A boy who can see spirits,
But that's no normal boy.

For at twilight, the blue figures appear,
Some of them are loud,
Some of them are shouty,
But one thing's for sure,
They all are quite messy.

Mikey Berry (12)
Penrice Academy, St Austell

My Roald Dahl Poem

Peter Puffin walked to the pier,
Peter Puffin jumped off the pier,
Peter Puffin went for a paddle,
Peter Puffin did not realise he was a seagull,
Peter was now called Cyril,
Seagull Cyril was written on his stone,
Seagull Cyril did not drown
Seagull Cyril flew into a drone.

Aaron Moss (12)
Penrice Academy, St Austell

The Wolf

The wolf is a thief, a liar of great order,
He is the best ever chaos-causer,
He's an excellent, brilliant, high-graded crook,
He doesn't even need the help of a book.

He has visited jail zero times,
He's got away with all his ninety-three crimes,
He's up in the day with the sunlight,
He takes home some meat to gobble at night.

He's a sneaky little liar and is wild,
He is a beast that loves to eat a big child
He's an extreme trickster, he's fast on his feet,
He's a cheeky rascal that loves to eat meat.

An encounter and you'll be running for the hills,
He is so strong that he blows down windmills
The wolf's a true thief, a really bad baddy,
He's stupendously quick, he can outrun your daddy.

He's got vicious and beady, well-seeing eyes
He's so stealthy that he can carry fifteen pies,
His brain is malevolent - a rampage of evil,
Once you are in him, you'll have no retrieval.

The wolf is a thief, a liar of great order,
Maybe though, he's not a chaos-causer,
He's probably now a mid-graded crook
Maybe he could now rely on a book.

Callum Reece Rooney (10)
Rice Lane Primary School, Liverpool

The Wolf

The wolf is a cheat, a liar and a thief
He always eats meat but has never touched beef
He likes to prank on every single child
But I guess he's not tamed so he's a little bit wild.

The wolf is extremely sly,
Too bad he has never caught a fly,
You can't go past him, not with his colossal feet,
When he sprints, he doesn't like to be beat.

When you meet the giant beast,
You'll scream and be his next feast!
He thinks he's a genius and a snob
But every day, we know he goes to rob.

When people are asleep,
The wolf goes to creep
He is a real crook
I couldn't count how many children he's took.

The wolf is a cheat, a liar and a thief
He always eats meat but has never touched beef
He likes to prank on every single child
But I guess he's not tamed so he's a little bit wild.

Mollie James (10)
Rice Lane Primary School, Liverpool

Wolfie

Wolfie is a cunning liar,
His eyes are blistering, sharp like fire,
He ate Grandma up in one big bite,
He sure didn't lose his appetite.

He's a feral stalker,
He's not much of a talker,
He's an imposter and a cheat,
He's ravenous when he doesn't eat.

He's malevolent and greedy,
He's sneaky and speedy,
He went and knocked on Grandma's door,
He scared her with a mighty roar.

He is aggressive and cruel
He really is a fool
He was shocked when he saw
The sharp, shiny saw.

Wolfie was a cunning liar
His eyes did blister, sharp like fire
He had eaten Grandma up in one big bite
He's now lost his appetite.

Sophie Elizabeth Greasley (10)
Rice Lane Primary School, Liverpool

Wolfy

Wolfy is a cunning liar,
His eyes are blistering, sharp like fire,
Little Red walked down the path,
Awaiting big, bad Wolfy's wrath.

They chatted lots, for evermore,
She led Wolfy to poor Granny's door,
He ate her up in one big bite,
The sly beast left that night.

He's a cruel phoney,
Who's quite moany,
He's a thief, a slacker, an evil tracker
He should be locked up for being a hacker.

He's a nasty cheat,
A brat, never neat
He's wild, he's feral,
And creates great peril.

Wolfy is a cunning liar,
His eyes are blistering, sharp like fire
Little Red walked down the path
Awaiting big, bad Wolfy's wrath.

Derry Aitken (11)
Rice Lane Primary School, Liverpool

The Wild Wolf

The wolf is a crook, a cheat and a baddy
He will eat your mummy, your nanny and your daddy.

He's extremely violent and also loves to slobber,
He always wants his way like a snob robber.

The big bad wolf is very wild
He is ready for dessert and that's your child.

He is a very sly wolf and a liar,
He is that poor, he doesn't care if he starts a fire.

The wolf is a trickster, like a wizard,
He always howls and makes a strong blizzard.

He needs a shower, to scrub his hair,
When he's done he'll eat you and your teddy bear.

The wolf is a crook, a cheat and a baddy
He will eat your mummy, your nanny and your daddy.

Jamie Tyrrell (10)
Rice Lane Primary School, Liverpool

The Wolf

The wolf is a cheat, a liar and a thief
He always eats meat but has never touched beef
He likes to prank on every single child
But I guess he's not tamed, so he's a little bit wild.

The wolf is extremely sly
Too bad he has never caught a fly
You can't go past him, not with his colossal feet
When he sprints, he doesn't like to be beat.

When you meet the giant beast,
You'll scream and be his next feast!
He thinks he's a genius and a snob
But every day, we know he goes to rob.

When people are asleep,
The wolf starts to creep,
He is a real crook,
I couldn't count how many children he's took.

Sophie Bowles (10)
Rice Lane Primary School, Liverpool

Wolfy

Wolfy is a cunning liar
He always stops to conspire
However, to everyone's annoyance and fright
He never seems to lose his appetite.

He's unlike the others
He has a better IQ
He didn't need a mother
His mind has a dark hue.

He zooms on his feet
Not so much with his wit
He's still not the smartest
He's still quite a twit.

He's once been killed
By the working lumberjack
In two his belly peeled
With a single, loud whack!

Ben Lawson (10)
Rice Lane Primary School, Liverpool

The Amazing Pineapple Story About Olivia And Unicorn Girl

Olivia is ten years old and Unicorn Girl is twenty. Olivia has blue eyes and Unicorn Girl has light blue eyes. She has black tights. Olivia has black tights too. Olivia has a blue bow, Unicorn Girl has white trainers and black shorts.

Unicorn Girl came to look after her. Then she saw something weird, it was a giant pineapple. So she asked Unicorn Girl to go in it. She said yes so they crawled in it. Olivia climbed in first. Then Unicorn Girl. They found a gearstick and were so excited, they started jumping. It started rolling faster, then there was a swimming pool.

"Look, there is a swimming pool!"

Olivia used her fire to melt a door and they went back home.

Nicole Barton
Sacred Heart RC Primary School, South Bretton

Jack And The Giant Strawberry

Lilly was an eight-year-old girl. Jack was seven years old.

One beautiful sunny day, Jack was playing in the garden. Suddenly, he saw a giant strawberry and then Lilly used her speed power. She ran after Jack. "Jack!" she shouted.

Lilly and Jack stepped inside it. It was dark and sticky. "Why do we have to go inside this strawberry?" said Lilly.

When they got to the centre, they saw a crystal heart Inside. Jack touched it and then it started to rock and roll. They were about to knock down the town, when it suddenly stopped. They quickly marched their way out. At last, they were free and ran home really fast.

Angeline Rose Caluducan (6)
Sacred Heart RC Primary School, South Bretton

A Mango Adventure

There were two girls and one was called Twilight and the other was called Rainbow Dash. And they were playing football but Rainbow Dash saw a big mango and Twilight ran to the mango and looked at how big it was. She pulled Rainbow Dash and pushed her in the mango! But there was no door. So Twilight magicked a door and walked in and saw a steering wheel. Twilight dropped the steering wheel and it started rolling. They were dizzy and Twilight used her magic to hold Rainbow Dash and stop the mango. But the door Twilight made, disappeared. So Twilight had to make another door and they flew out and saw they were home and went to their families.

Sithabile (Star) Mtisi
Sacred Heart RC Primary School, South Bretton

Red Nose And The Giant Apple

Once upon a time, there was Red Nose and Tom. Red Nose was twenty and Tom was ten. It was Red Nose's job to look after Tom. Tom was playing in the garden. Tom saw a giant, juicy apple. Red Nose went after him. Tom knocked the gearstick and the apple started moving. The apple was heading towards the shop. The apple squashed all the food and Red Nose said, "What are we going to do?"
"I don't know," said Tom.
Tom had an idea.
"Let's teleport back home," said Tom.
They teleported back home and they fell asleep. When Red Nose and Tom woke, their parents were home.

Adrian Kuszyk (6)
Sacred Heart RC Primary School, South Bretton

The Amazing, Wonderful Story About Roise And Mell

Roise is seven and Mell is ten. Roise was getting ready for school, she put a bobby pin in her hair. Suddenly, there was a huge pineapple. Mell woke up. Roise went in the pineapple. Mell jumped so high. It rolled faster, it took them to the North Pole.
Mell said, "We need a plan."
Roise said, "I have a bobby pin in my hair."
Mell said, "Yeah, that will do."
Roise took her bobby pin out.
Roise said, "I can cut a door."
Mell said, "Yes."
Roise cut a door and they jumped and landed on their feet. The pineapple was in the stall.

Tayla Nicholls (7)
Sacred Heart RC Primary School, South Bretton

Flisty And The Giant Raspberry

One day, Flisty and Ethel had a race to the playground. Ethel had blonde hair and a black bow. Flisty had a blue, red and white jacket and also, black boots.
Flisty saw a raspberry on a bouncy thing and Flisty thought she would munch her way through it and the raspberry said, "Five, four, three, two, one..." Blast off! Raspberries were falling from the sky and it bounced on the airport and it bounced all the way home and they were laughing all the way home but there was one thing bad, they didn't want to jump but the raspberry landed all by itself and they felt very dizzy and ran home.

Julia Anna Maliborska (7)
Sacred Heart RC Primary School, South Bretton

Shadowdash And Fireboy's Massive Pineapple

Fireboy was practising swimming in the garden. Later, Fireboy spotted a massive pineapple. Fireboy started nibbling the top of the pineapple before Shadowdash could stop him going into the pineapple. Fireboy saw a steering wheel and a gearstick. The pineapple started moving and it went full speed.

It cracked the fence, it was going to crash into a massive house. Shadowdash had to crawl really slowly so he didn't bump his head. When he came out, he was covered in giant pineapple juice. Fireboy crawled after Shadowdash, he was covered in ginormous pineapple pieces, all stuck in his hair.

Joshua Antony Jose (7)
Sacred Heart RC Primary School, South Bretton

Elly And The Giant Orange

Elly has a nice dress, pink shoes and shorts. She saw a giant orange and she munched her way in. Inside the giant orange, she saw a big steering wheel and she touched it. The giant orange rolled to a kid's swimming pool. Elly saw her mum by the pool who was looking for her.

They teleported away from a giant orange and Elly's mum said, "If you see a giant fruit again, just leave it!" She said sorry to her mum and promised to not do it again. Her mum said it was okay and they made their way home hoping not to see a giant fruit again.

Sigrid Elizabeth Avenido (7)
Sacred Heart RC Primary School, South Bretton

The Gigantic Pineapple

Benny was on his way to school and he found a gigantic pineapple and munched it.
Silver flew in afterwards. Silver found a big blue button and she tripped and slammed it. The pineapple started rolling, she accidentally pressed it and it started to roll faster and faster. It was heading for the town fair. What could they do?
They pressed the same button and it finally stopped. Benny has scissors in his pencil case and cut a door on the left side then jumped across the bridge to school. Silver followed.

Lyla Agnes Cronin (6)
Sacred Heart RC Primary School, South Bretton

Ava And The Giant Pineapple

One day, Ava and Lewis were playing in the garden when they saw a giant pineapple, they were shocked. They went in the pineapple and Ava munched it. Ava and Lewis were in there. Ava and Lewis didn't like it that much. Ava and Lewis were really, really scared. The pineapple kept on moving. When the pineapple stopped moving, Ava remembered a knife in her pocket. So Ava cut a door. Ava and Lewis were really, really happy. Ava and Lewis jumped out of the pineapple. Ava and Lewis walked and walked to the beach.

Liliana
Sacred Heart RC Primary School, South Bretton

An Amazing Story

One day, Red Ninger and Blue Ninger were playing in the garden. They turned around and saw a big apple. Blue Ninger saw Red going inside the apple. Blue Ninger stopped him. Red Ninger said that he wanted to go inside it and then Blue Ninger said that he wanted to go inside it.

Red Ninger pressed a green button and then it went faster and it went over the fence. It went over the road and drove to the hotel. Red Ninger used his sharp knife and cut the top off the apple and never did it again.

Gianluca
Sacred Heart RC Primary School, South Bretton

The Story About Mr Silmin

Mr Silmin had to look after his brother so he went to play in the garden. They saw an apple and ate it. Then the apple started to roll 'til it hit something unusual and they said, "We have to move."
They had a plan. The plan was to teleport and it worked. They were so happy they tried to move it but it didn't work because it was so heavy. It was the end of Mr Silmin and the giant apple that rolled 900 miles an hour.

Oscar James Cornell (7)
Sacred Heart RC Primary School, South Bretton

Emma And The Giant Apple

Emma was eight years old. One sunny day when Emma was playing in the untidy garden, she saw a giant apple. And then the giant apple started rolling all the way to the park. The giant apple rolled to the park and it suddenly stopped. Emma felt dizzy and banged her head. They munched their way out and jumped off the top.

Cheska Caragay
Sacred Heart RC Primary School, South Bretton

The Bread Factory

As Joseph stepped into the spacy room, his eyes moved east to see a crowd of holey and spongy mountains made of sponge cake. He stepped off the stairs and waded his feet in the wheat. The fans made his hair dance in the air. In front of him were gallons of fresh golden wheat. A delicious smell wafted through the room. The smell of bread. All he could hear was the sound of the twirling fans.

He ventured off to the cream dispenser, staring. He watched as the white, soft cream came out. He licked it. It was so flavoursome. He had a vision of the workers working away upstairs. The rocky ground under him felt like a billion minute mounds. He trudged up to the fondue pond. There were sticks and bread in front of him. He followed a small path leading to the raisin trees. Once a year, they exploded the raisins off for the bread. Next to them, lined up were many ovens and breadmakers each working away. He lay down and looked up. He could see the reflection of the wheat in the mirrors.

Julia Reiter
Shirley Community Primary School, Cambridge

The Doughnut Factory

As Charlie opened the door, he gazed around to see all of Willy Wonka's creations. He thought, *is this really happening?* Charlie was nervous, what if he ate something because he wouldn't be able to resist it? What if he touched something and it broke? As he looked up, he saw the banana and white chocolate fudge sun, it was so blazing the light wanted to bounce off it. The salt cloud was dropping salt off all the chocolate, it was weird but quite a tasty combination. There was everything! Charlie tried to sniff the smell out of the floating gingerbread house alarm and he could hear the condiment waterfall splashing on the hot dogs. The smell was spreading across the room like fresh ink out of a pen but Charlie could just smell pure dreams and the doughnuts he saw spinning were as gold as a brushed Corgi's fur. The rice paper plates and gummy bear cups were great, you wouldn't have to wash the dishes. Charlie thought the icing pond was amazing!

Sophia Herriot
Shirley Community Primary School, Cambridge

Mary And The Pasta Factory

As Mary skipped into the pasta garden, her heart was beating rapidly. She saw cute, fluffy Footfooty security in the left top corner, making sure there were no intruders!

To the right of the Footfooty, lay a macaroni mushroom. *Wow! Isn't that amazing?* Suddenly, Mary spied two spaghetti trees with spaghetti dangling down the trunk. She loved the runny cheese pond next to the macaroni mushroom.

Her eyes caught the eggs exploding near the chicken farm. Close to that there was a cooking place with the stove flaming like mad. The eggs travelled through a tube where the other ingredients were added. It was sent to the pasta shaper where the pasta was formed. Beside the pasta shaper, there lay the pasta deliverer taking uncooked pasta to the cooking station. In the far corner were two fusilli dispensers, pushing fusilli out into purple, shiny and patterned bowls.

Elena Hazel Southall
Shirley Community Primary School, Cambridge

Charlie And The Chocolate Factory

The door opened to the colossal factory! There was a sudden silence, Charlie looked around him. He could clearly see that everybody was discombobulated, speechless. Who knows what they were thinking? To Charlie's left, he saw fizzing waterfalls filled with candy, sweets, all types of things that were yummy.

There was the man who changed the world of chocolate, the man was gleaming. Charlie smelt a sweet aroma coming from the ceiling. There was a blanket of dangling candyfloss, to be accurate, chocolate candyfloss clouds standing as still as an iron cage. When Charlie looked to the right, he saw a chocolate fountain. He tasted a bit of the spraying chocolate, it was phenomenal. His eyes could see the dream he had been dreaming of ever since he was four, so this was once in a lifetime. It was a memory he would treasure forever...

Roberta May Rayner (9)
Shirley Community Primary School, Cambridge

The Appetising Pizza Factory

As Charlie walked into the factory, he was amazed, gobsmacked, discombobulated. He beamed at the warm cheese waterfall, as the fizz-whizzing toppings of a pizza came falling down. Next to it was a field of junk food with burgers, chicken nuggets, fries and pizza trees with pizzas on them! Right on the other side of the room, there was sauce spreading like an infection. The sauce changed every two seconds you tasted it. Under was a group of pigs in blankets. Oh how Charlie loved the taste of pigs in blankets, especially at Christmas... and some curry! The pigs in blankets rolled around a pool of curry as if they were alive! Charlie slowly lost the grip of his grandad's hand as he scanned the factory room. It was what he had dreamed of.

Sean Pungorn Richardson (9)
Shirley Community Primary School, Cambridge

Shruti And The Incredible Ice Cream Factory

As Shruti gazed around the ice cream factory, she caught a glimpse of the whizzing topping machine with buttons you didn't need to push to activate which was beyond the never-ending, giant pink marshmallow. There was a satisfying, squishy trampoline right next to the never-ending marshmallow and on its left, there was a speedy, flying unicorn.

Curiously, Shruti continued into the factory, wondering what would appear around the next corner. Then she could smell something incredibly delicious coming up her nose - it was coming from the centre of the colossal room - it was the creamy, milky waterfall and next to it was a lollipop with whizz-popping colours and flavours.

Shruti Saha
Shirley Community Primary School, Cambridge

Albert And The Amazing Spaghetti Factory

As Albert entered the vast room, he stopped and glared at the room. He could see a butter waterfall! Underneath the waterfall was massive, gigantic toast with boiling melted butter on it. Albert could also see a spaghetti volcano with blazing, boiling sauce slithering down!

The next thing he saw was a melted, creamy cheese fountain mixed with butter. Next to the fountain, there was a white cup that you needed to scoop up the melted, slimy cheese and drink it. Albert felt amazed! He had lots of feelings in one.

Slowly, Albert turned his back for one second and gazed at the astonishing, incredible, infinite meatball mountain, where if you eat a meatball, it comes back!

Albert
Shirley Community Primary School, Cambridge

Charlie And The Amazing Sweet Factory

As Charlie entered the huge room, he smelt the sweet aroma of juicy, crispy bacon. He caught sight of over 100,000 sweets which were everywhere! He walked to his left and smelt salted chocolate that was sweet as a box! Charlie tasted some. He heard the cheese sauce river sizzle like a sausage. The icy candy clouds were raining exquisite candies and Charlie loved the factory. Charlie heard the river bubbling and he saw the Oompa-Loompas. They were working hard. Charlie travelled to the cheese sauce river and tasted the cheese sauce river that was flowing like a volcano. Gumballs came out of the delicious, sweet-smelling roof.

Joseph Owen Nathaniel Stewart (8)
Shirley Community Primary School, Cambridge

Charlie's Sweet Adventure

As Charlie gazed around the vast room, the first article that he saw was the sweet, round, waffle mountain. It looked so flavoursome. He ran to it and took one to eat. When he was finished, he saw the whipped cream volcano. After that, he gaped at the long, silky chocolate river. He would just love to swim in it. But Charlie went straight to the jolly jumper because it looked super bouncy and tasty. When he jumped, he went higher than the marshmallow clouds! Just then, his tummy rumbled so he trekked to the pancake waterfall. He grabbed three pancakes and went to the honey waterfall.

Orrin
Shirley Community Primary School, Cambridge

Charlie And The Cereal Factory

As young Charlie entered the vast room, guess what he saw? Millions of marshmallow people greeting them! He wandered further in and smelt the essence of milk and cereal and saw a huge waterfall, it was gushing loudly and he could hear boulders falling off trees. This was the best day of Charlie's life.

"The factory is the best place ever!" Charlie exclaimed as he chewed a boulder.

Next, he stared at the cookie crisp mountain in amazement. Next, he decided to climb the box wall and as it turned to night, he slowly fell asleep...

Jemima Graves
Shirley Community Primary School, Cambridge

Edward And The Everything Factory!

As Edward looked around the vast room, he saw frosting rain. Behind him were the strawberry lollipops. To his left, he could see space sweets popping like stars. After a while, Edward began to hear strawberry sprinkles splatting onto the floor. The sound of sticky bubblegum came from under his feet. The aroma of grass began to tickle his nose. Edward reached forward and grabbed a tube of bubblegum. He could taste McDonald's burgers as he chewed.
Edward said, "This is cool!"

Edward
Shirley Community Primary School, Cambridge

Girl

This is the story which is about a sister of a boy called Boy. Her name is Girl, she is a sibling of five. Their names are Goginy, aged fifteen; Bogo, aged eight; Boy, aged thirteen; Trogbox, aged twenty-three and Girl, aged twelve. She goes to an ordinary school and has an ordinary home but what happens in the home is not ordinary. They have self-cleaning plates and self-tidying beds. Their house sets them apart from normal people. They also speak Gobbletin. They only speak Gobbletin when they are alone or trying to address something private or important.

One normal day, Girl awoke and went downstairs and found a note saying, 'Meet me at Whizzpop at 10:30am sharp. We need to address something in Gobbletin'. Girl and Boy were the only ones in the whole house. That meant only one thing, party time. They grabbed all the alcohol and chocolate before you could think. The party was a blast, lots of shots and lots of chocolate.

Thirty minutes later...

"Ah, my intestines feel like they are giving birth," Boy mumbled whilst lying on the ground.

On the other side of the house, Girl was standing over the toilet, throwing up her organs into a bowl of water. Then, she remembered the letter.

"Oi Boy, drive me to Whizzpop or you will get a free snack, a knuckle sandwich!" Girl screamed at Boy. Boy grabbed the car keys and raced to Whizzpop like a Nascar driver. When they got to the destination, it changed her life...

Ollie Lawson (11)
St John's College, Southsea

Turkey Trouble

Last week Farmer Bertie sat in his field as the snow fell down. "Oh, stop this gropswatting snow!" he yelled. "I'm chilled to the bone."
It was as cold as a billion freezers in a tiny room. Farmer Bertie was a cranky old drunkard despised by all the village children. This Christmas especially he didn't want to share his turkeys with anyone. So this is why he was sitting on a deckchair with his pipe and a gun.
A mile away in the village, William and a few of the other village children, David, George and Peter, were preparing for a raid.
"We've got to get one this time," William moaned.
They set off and soon reached the farm. Peter hurled a test tube down on the farmstead.
"Mum's gravy," he muttered.
"What's that shoe-shooting noise?" a voice cried from below.
The children ran to the turkey sheds and picked the lock. The farmer burst in and chucked his pipe on the floor. Side-stepping, all the children stepped out the door. The farmer chucked turkeys at them met by vials of gravy and cranberry sauce. The chase persisted on past the geese who honked as they passed into the collapsed farmhouse. Farmer Bertie trod on his gun, the liqueur exploded catching the trees alight.

Farmer Bertie catapulted to the moon as a pre-roasted turkey fell into each child's hands. They walked to the Christingle service happily.

Matthew Poole (11)
St John's College, Southsea

Halloween

It was on one Halloween on a very spooky night when Michal was scoffing all the sweets he got from trick or treating. The sweets he ate were Mars bars fudge and gubblefunk. Gubblefunk is a chocolate bar, made out of nougat but whilst he was eating his last bar, he heard a noise.

It was a quiet echoing bellow which said, "Save me." The minute he heard the cry for help he passed up the stairs but by the time he got upstairs there was nothing there. He searched everywhere to find out where the noise came from but the more he searched the louder the voice echoed, to the point where it was unbearable and he fainted, which triggered the secret lair and he ragdoll-slid down the stairs.

By the time he woke up, he wondered where he was. He was on a pedestal surrounded by lava and there was a locked door. He wondered if his locked door would take him home. Behind him there was a monkey bar parkour. If he made one false step he would fall into the lava. He lurched forward...

Adam Peter Brumder (13)
St John's College, Southsea

The Flabbergasting Wonderful World Of Roald Dahl

Roald Dahl was a phizz-whizzing wizard,
He created whole new magical worlds filled with wonder and remarkability,
Charlie, Matilda and James were some of his characters,
Many generations of children loved his books,
Authors of all shapes and sizes were inspired by him,
He took part in the war many others did too,
He saved many lives,
With fighting and with books,
He was born in Wales but his parents were Norwegian,
His teachers said he was no good in school,
Ha ha ha!
What a bunch of fools,
He was a giant at six-foot-six,
He must've had his Weetabix,
You'd think Willy Wonka was a character,
But no, Willy's a postman from Nebraska,
He made over 250 new words,
He loved power drills, chocolate and snooker cues,
And his HB pencils too.

Nuhad Zaman (12)
St John's College, Southsea

The Extramentous Adventure Of Fig

There once was a boy called Fig,
He lived in a very large dig,
But one day someone said,
"Oi Fig, you've got no head."
Then Fig had to go on an adventure,
And hope he didn't have to get some dentures.
On his ginormous walk,
He needed someone to talk,
So he went to the local pub,
And he had a good chug,
But didn't find anyone to help,
So he went to have a yelp,
Then a young fellow lad,
Came, said, "Are you sad?"
Then this boy and Fig were good friends,
But they met lots of dead ends,
Though they never gave up,
They eventually found a cup,
It read, 'Whoever drinks this instead,
Will regrow a head'.
Then Fig drank this,
And the head came to be his.

Enzo Richardson (12)
St John's College, Southsea

Matilda

M indful of all her friends and family
A mazing supernatural powers to control anything.
T houghtful of others and is not afraid to stick up for what she believes in.
I s mischievous and likes to be a little bit naughty.
L oves to read and goes to the library most days, is very friendly with the librarian, Mrs Phelps.
D etermined to succeed in life no matter what gets in her way.
A dored by her lovely teacher, Miss Honey, who has an open heart to all her students.

Grace Hooper (12)
St John's College, Southsea

BFG's Thoughts

A few gulps of Frobscottle makes me feel hopscotchy,
I engorged all the Snozzcumbers ever so cheerlessly,
All these foods I really don't like,
But then I remember I never want to eat children alike,
All the other giants who would eat any child in sight,
It doesn't matter whether they are large or thin and it isn't based on their height,
This makes me feel sick and fills me with fear,
Sophie, this brave girl has to get out of here.

Sophia Baxter (12)
St John's College, Southsea

Roald Dahl Poem

Matilda the book lover
Michael her rude mean brother
Bruce the cake monster
Miss Honey the loving teacher.

The Big Friendly Giant
Always being there for Jody
Helping him on his journeys
The giant catching his dreams.

Charlie the lucky boy
Veruca always begging
Mike TeaVee the gamer boy
Violet always chewing
Into the factory there they go
Where a surprise happens and they don't know.

Elyza Jan Parazo (14)
St John's College, Southsea

Roald Dahl's Books

James made a giant peach with lots of little potions,
The Twits never washed their hair with shampoo or lotion.
Fantastic Mr Fox was clever and sly,
Esio Trot just wanted to fly.
Emo had the magic finger,
In their home, The Twits would linger.
Zip zip zap!
Wip wip wap!
The BFG was very tall,
Charlie was quite small.

Finley George Steele (11)
St John's College, Southsea

My Dad's Flying Pig

A few years ago, my dad said he would buy a flying pig. We all said, "That's fine," thinking that he wouldn't. So my dad got into his van to get his flying pig. When he was away, our neighbour had pulled into her house in a gold Rolls Royce and when she got out, Miss Dinosaur was wearing gold all around her body. Then one day, the police came and arrested her for robbing the bank. When my dad came home, there was a big, fat animal.

When he got into the house, we all stared at him and asked him, "What is that?"

He told us it was his flying pig.

We were really confused then he said, "It's dead."

We all asked him, "How did he die?"

He replied, "The heat in the van must have killed it."

I guess the moral of the story is don't keep a pig in heat for too long.

Christy Meegan (10)
St Patrick's Primary School, Eskra

Granny's Knickers

Granny had a pair of frilly knickers. She loved them so much she never had washed them before. She wanted to keep them for all her life. One day when she woke up, she realised she had no knickers on... They were gone!

Granny screamed, "Who dares to take my knickers?" She jumped out of bed and I dare not say she had no knickers on. She put on a plaid dress and big black boots and went on a search for her frilly knickers. She searched her son's house first but no! Not there. She searched her neighbours, but alas, not there! She searched everywhere! No, not anywhere.

She screamed, "Who took my frilly knickers?"

She went home sad and plopped on her bed and said, "Oh, I need to get a pair of new knickers."

She went outside and what was there? You'll never guess, her frilly knickers up a pole!

Berneen Gilroy (10)
St Patrick's Primary School, Eskra

Delumptious

- **D** elicious
- **E** xtra-usual
- **L** oved
- **U** nbelievable
- **M** agnificent
- **P** erfect
- **T** eatime
- **I** mpossibly amazeballs
- **O** ver the top
- **U** cky-mucky
- **S** pag bol.

Phoebe Ryle (13)
The County High School, Leftwich

The Sinister Lights

Felicia couldn't sleep, throughout the town of Goggleworth, she was solemnly sitting all on her own, looking out of a window in an orphanage.

Throughout the time she had been there, she had seen no end of people from far away come in and out of the old, unwanted, grotesque house which stood at the top of the Goggleworth Hill, peering over the petite town. She wished and wondered every single day and night that she could live an extravagant and enthusiastic life with a family. She could do whatever she wanted when she wanted and would live a super-duper life.

It was March 2065 and there was still no luck of her being chosen. She was petrified of being in the orphanage for years to come. Tragic things had happened when she was a youngster. She had been through the most horrific life. Whilst she was with her parents, she had somehow managed to misplace them whilst at the market of Dinkleborough.

Tons and tons of thoughts had gone through her head. What happens if they were dead? What if they had forgotten about her? What if they were in a different country?

Then one day, she woke up like somebody had punched her. *Bang! Crash! Wallop!* She jolted up and looked around the room. Everybody was fast asleep, snoring. She peered through the window and looked outside. She wondered why nobody had been disturbed and woken up by the screeching noise that was outside. She went downstairs to the scullery for a drink of water, and guzzled a cupful down.

She ran back up to the dormitory and everyone had disappeared. Where had they gone? Who had taken them? She looked out the window and noticed flashing lights coming towards the house. Felicia allowed her eyes to travel further and further down the street. Suddenly, she hesitated. Who was it? Were they coming for her?

Lucy Tunnicliffe (12)
The Wigston Academies Trust, Wigston

Aliens

Bob McBobbob is a very unusual two-year-old. The first reason is, he has already passed all the school tests and has a university degree in chemistry, physics, maths, English, biology, geography and history. Also, he owns a multibillion-pound business, Bobbycorp, which is the leading business in technology. The final reason is, he is the cleverest person alive.

On the day our story starts, Bob and his parents are on his super bounce trampoline when a strange UFO appears in the sky, turning his mother and father to goo. Then drops a claw, scooping up Bob. Inside the UFO are a bunch of red and slimy aliens. They all speak in croaky voices. "We are the aliens of Smugwul and we will turn you into yummy, gooey food."

At that time, Bob notices that there are more children with him. He sits down next to a kid who looks about ten.

"Eho," says the boy. "Me Dave, me in year one school."

"Shut up, you slimy, little ooden," says an alien.

Now Bob is scared. A plan forms in Bob's mind, he sees that they are approaching Smugwul, he also sees a sign saying: *Planet destroying choglo beam*, and knows it means laser beam...

Woody Orton (12)
The Wigston Academies Trust, Wigston

Ben And The Wonderful Plane

I am Ben and this is what I do in my spare time! In my backyard is a hangar and in that hangar is a desk and beside my desk is a... plane. Yes, that is right, a plane! Every evening when the sky turns a magical, purplish orange I linger about in the hangar and reconstruct the antique plane. Every so often you can hear a bang or a bong and the deafening silence. Some days I lose hope, not today!

I finally manage to fix the engine after long hours of assiduous work. As soon as I can I take off. My heart beats like a drum. We start to cross the Atlantic! A cumulonimbus starts to sprout like a venomous mushroom and I know that I must go full throttle but it will destroy the rusty engine. Desperately, looking around, I reach across the plane and nimbly press a large, velvet coloured button. Straining to stay in my seat, the plane lurches forward and I gaze at the wonderful view of New York. Central Park is a mosaic of colours from a bird's eye view as all the flowers join together as if it is a puzzle.

By now, I am starting to ask myself the real question... Where do I land? Scrutinising the area, I find a large field near the Empire State building. Finally landing, I tell myself ecstatically, "This is it, I've made it!"

Alexandre Nasser (11)
Wetherby Senior School, London

Mr Marabou And The Chocolate Mayhem

One fresh autumn morning, chocoholic Mr Marabou, the mad, bonkers chemistry teacher, had reached his 11th year of teaching at White House School. I should probably mention here that Mr Marabou is a unique teacher: he is a horse - a suit-wearing, fast-thinking English-speaking genius horse with a deep love of chocolates, chemistry and chemicals.

Today's lesson was packed full with Periodic Table facts and important lab rules, oh and... chocolate chat, of course! During the lesson, Mr Marabou began dreaming of creating a brand-new scrumptious chocolate: a Marabou bar! Without realising, he began to dribble and drool in front of the Year 7 students. He then suddenly snapped out of his hazy chocolate dream and exclaimed, "It's break time!" All students were dismissed and hurriedly cleared out of the science lab; everyone running to next lessons and fixtures. With the coast clear, Mr Marabou decided there and then to conduct a chocolate practical to develop his fabulous Mr Marabou bar.

How would he make this new and amazing treat? His clever superbrain began whizzing and fizzing through all of the possible chocolate combinations, his horse mane flicking from side to side with adrenaline and excitement.

"Aha! That's it! Magic! I have the answer!" he exclaimed, excitedly twitching in delight. "A superior, ultimate bar of chocolate, concocted and precisely mixed, containing all of my top 100 favourite treats!" He swung open his briefcase in which he kept the secret stash of his favourite sweet, creamy and nutty chocolates. As quick as a flash, he gathered together his equipment, lit the bunsen burner and clunked his hooves together, rubbing them with joy.

"Melt a gram of this, stir a bit of that, mix a few of those, pour this, sprinkle those, dip that and frost the lot!" An excited and happy snort came from his hairy nostrils. "It is done!"

A marvellous Marabou bar lay on the counter in front of his bulging, hungry eyes. He picked up the gorgeous bar with his milk chocolate hooves and gobbled it up in one fast bite, leaving only a speck behind, his dark eyes closed as if he were in heaven, his horsey ears twitching in bliss.

All of a sudden, the school bell rang which instantly woke him up from his chocolate coma. Mr Marabou raced around the lab tidying the evidence away and busying himself to pack up so that he could race home and record the results of this epic experiment. Removing his custom lab coat, revealing his brown spotted necktie and pink striped suit, he spun around with a horsey neigh and grabbed his chocolate-stuffed briefcase and there, before him, sitting proudly on the table, where the speck of Marabou Bar lay was another, perfectly-formed Marabou Bar... just like the original!

"How can this be? Regeneration! A magical mystery? A miracle? A never-ending chocolate bar?"
This autumn morning had turned out to be the best morning *ever* for a chocoholic horse like Mr Marabou!

Oscar Jaworski (11)
Wetherby Senior School, London

Doomsday

We had done it. We pulled it off!

The greatest prank in the school's history and we got away with it. We got away with it... for about eight seconds. Our original plan was to sneak past the school security and manage to get into the camera room. We managed to mould a fake key that only had one use before it broke.

As we opened the door we were greeted by an empty security room! Thatcher quickly walked up to the school intercom, the rest of us gazing up at the CCTV cameras that covered every nook and cranny of the entire campus. Thatcher pushed down the red button, meaning his voice could go live to the whole school when he spoke.

"I am your father," he said in a booming Darth Vadar voice. But, we didn't realise that the whole school would hear it... not just the students.

Before we knew it we were surrounded by teachers and a red-faced, sweaty security guard. We all shuffled our feet and looked down at the ground as we waited for the yelling to ensue. After the drill-sergeant-like lecture was over we were grabbed by the arms and pushed through a door. There we were, in the headmaster's office.

The office had a nice homely feel to it, the floor tiles were a dark oak wood and a carpet covered it. Two neatly placed chairs overlooked a rather petite table with a porcelain tea set. But our eyes were quickly diverted to a rather messy desk where the headmaster

sat. He was a rather slim man but he was tall at about six foot two. He looked down on us as we stood at the hilt of his desk, he didn't look too happy.

"You boys embarrassed the whole school while visitors were around, do you have anything to say for yourselves?" For a slim man, the headmaster had a booming voice and the rest of the staff exited the office.

"Uuuum... no... sir," Thatcher mumbled. We were all shaking. Everyone who had come out of his office looked frightened. This was our first run-in with him so maybe he'd have mercy?

No. He had no mercy. We were all suspended for a week and on top of that, we had to apologise to the visitors present at the school, which was quite embarrassing. The teachers hated us now. We would always be picked out by them in lessons and let's just say that after that prank the school's reputation for being a highly academic place for learning was ruined. But it was definitely worth it.

Billy Carter (11)
Wetherby Senior School, London

The Prank

One plain and ordinary Monday school morning - Max, Jonathan, Matty and I had had enough of the same old exhausting ritual of dragging ourselves into another day of Mr Plympton's history class. Matty threw a squinting glance at our group of friends; you know when he is up to no good. His glance suggested he was up to no good at all. Matty was in detention weekly for doing sneaky and sly pranks; he was always in trouble twenty-four-seven. Mr Plympton was our stiff, robotic and uninteresting history teacher. We detested him with all of our hearts.

As usual, we entered the classroom for our lesson, but surprisingly Mr Plympton was not there. There was something on his desk. Lying on the table was a mass of hair that looked like a wig...

"Hmm... I wonder what this could be?" said Matty.

"Hold on. Are you thinking what I'm thinking?" I said.

Matty tried on this giant, hideous fur ball on his tiny head. We heard trembling footsteps shaking the ground. He was caught red-handed by Mr Plympton. That was when we (well mainly him) wanted sweet revenge on our rotten history teacher. We were going to steal his toupee. Everyone, now I mean everybody, in school thought that Mr Plympton had lots of hair, but no, oh no my friend he didn't. So we did it. We wanted to show that school we aren't just a group of boring old nerds.

After an exhausting and tedious day of schoolwork, we waited for two hours so that every single teacher could leave the building. Those hours felt like years. I don't know how we possibly survived it, but we did. Once the time came after the teachers finished writing gibberish on the pupils' work, we finally got to his office. Mr Plympton's office specifically. Getting to his office was just like in the movies. We snuck underneath the doors, ran quietly through the building, zigzagged through numerous booby traps, all as silent as a whisper. Not one sound, just silence. Then we got to his office.
The tension in the air was surreal. The flaming sweat trickling down our sticky and slimy faces oozed with disgust. Thoughts were racing past our minds eccentrically, and we couldn't keep track of them. Yet we still did it. Max carried the giant leather bag, Johnathan held the beaming flashlight, and Matty was the spy, keeping track of everything happening around us. You know, we weren't a popular group of people, but doing this made us feel bigger than any other person in the school. We felt popular for the first time in forever. Whilst thinking of our massive achievement, we silently tiptoed outside of the office, and we just had one last check to see if we'd forgotten anything, you know, just in case. I high-high-fived all my mates with a victory. It was a success. Luckily we didn't forget anything.

But it turns out he wasn't the only one with a toupee. We'd just stolen the toupee belonging to our headmaster, Mr Horriblis...

Elijah Newman (11)
Wetherby Senior School, London

The Magic TV Remote

I woke up this morning to a surprise. Our TV remote had changed colour. It shone an aubergine-purple shade and it had all sorts of buttons etched into its rough surface. The strange device had one button that could take you to a land of sweets and chocolate. Another could take you to bleak, inhospitable surroundings.

I selected a unique golden button titled, 'The Fountain' and, taking care not to put too much pressure on the button, I pressed it and everything went black. I woke up to a harmonious tune and I suddenly saw the beautiful environment that captured my longing gaze. The ground was a shimmering white tint and snowflakes fell around my knees. An immense fountain stood proud.

I managed to pull myself away and I teleported to a land of sweets. A massive candy cane was pushed into the ground and a lake of melting chocolate caught my eyes, I took a mouthful and it was the greatest experience ever.

Before I could eat anything else, I transported myself to the bleak, inhospitable surroundings I had seen on the remote earlier. It had a pale-yellow floor with great lumps of light-blue rocks jutting out of the ground like dead roots from a dying tree. Golden specks fell to the ground, landing with a soft touch.

Suddenly, I was teleported back to my living room and I was so exhausted that I jumped onto the sofa and fell asleep.

Alistair Rountree (10)
Willingham Primary School, Willingham

Ella

Ella was a little girl. She lived in a massive city with her great-uncle Eric. Uncle Eric was a small old man with a slateshine bald head and a long, wispy, white beard. He had eyes which seemed to look right through you and a pinched face. Her uncle was a cruel man who made her dust every nook and cranny of his palace-like home. She had to get up at one o'clock. If she didn't, at exactly six o'clock, she'd get whipped. Her bedroom was a small room, there was not even enough room for a bed, just a thin blanket and no pillow. It was around the size of a cupboard.

One day, on the way back from school, she was being bullied. She stared aggressively at the three boys and then they were gone. She looked down and saw three frogs. From then on, after school, she took a detour through the woods to practise her sorcery. A few weeks later, she was standing outside the shower and this time, she stared angrily. What came out of the shower was not old Uncle Eric. Oh no! It was a snake. A green, slimy snake. Ella immediately dialled the zoo's number. The next second, he was in a zoo. And for Ella, well, her friends took her in and she's now part of the Nightwind family.

Jenny May Slater (9)
Willingham Primary School, Willingham

Roald Dahl

R idiculously funny stories
O bviously amazing tales
A wesome characters!
L ooking... and can't stop
D oes a unique job!

D ream a little dream
A mazing work with the stories
H ungry for more
L oving the books!

Nia Lily Rose Mills (9)
Willingham Primary School, Willingham

My Poem About Roald Dahl

R eading master
O n top of it
A te some children
L aughing genius
D readful Twits.

D reaming about it
A musing stories
H appiness is found
L onging for Dahl's books.

Isla Hayes (9)
Willingham Primary School, Willingham

The Eraow

A young boy set off
In his gleaming chevestic
Although people scoff
He certainly looked majestic.

Away from his home werradith
He looks forward yonder
This Eraow is not a myth
Was what he ponders.

He took upon this novaly
All on his own
His mother prays hopefully
He does not return in bones.

The Eraow was an ancient story
A massive winged beast snores
Only one can win all the glory
If Eraow is slain, all riches are yours.

But the boy did not venture
To slaughter the mighty beast
He did not want the treasures
Instead, he and Eraow made peace.

Hang Tran (13)
Woodside High School, Wood Green

Zingtra Mountain War

There once was a war in the Zingtra Mountains,
Over the gracious and elegant Zingtra Fountain,
It granted the valiant from a wish to a cure,
But to do so they needed a heart so pure,
On one side was the skilled and wise Sheluka,
On the other, the ferocious and reckless Ontruka,
When both Xojes sounded, the war was underway,
And what began a minor argument, was now an affray...
Sheluka Quintelopi came from above,
While Ontruka Vucus charged with a trusty Mintrika glove,
Many fighters were stabbed and crushed 'til they were non-existent,
But both sides had hope and both were persistent,
After hours and hours, there was only a handful left of Sheluka,
And a handful left of brotherly Ontruka,
Both leaders, however, still remained,
Eager to find out what the Zingtra Fontain contained...
But both were blinded by anger and greed,
With a sudden urge to conquer and succeed,
They weren't ready and weren't mature,
Neither had a heart that was warm and pure,

And all of a sudden appeared a blinding light,
Shining and illuminating the darkest night,
A figure arose with a heart so pure,
With the sacred sword of Willudure,
Once both sides realised, the Sheluka and Ontruka,
Bolted to hug their long-lost father, the Peruka...
They were glad that the fountain brought back their father for intervening,
It gave back friendship its meaning,
Tranquillity took its place,
The war was over...

Charles William Laurence (13)
Woodside High School, Wood Green

The Best Day Ever

Today, I had a very bad slepable

Because I was jogampo, a game called the Double Bubble

My dad apera me up at seven o'clock to go to school

It was non-uniform day, so I dressed in my best rupa to look cool

By period three, Mr Carlos wanted to give me a carat for a trip

Because I had won second place in competition for the best spaceship

The trip was to Thorpe Park

And my best compeca was going with me, his name is Clark

It was going to be on the 5th of May

And that's on my birthday!

Today is my birthday, I couldn't slepabol the whole night

Yesterday, I came from Spain and it was a bad flight

My dad took me to school and my compeca, Clark, was waiting for me

It was 7.30am, we were going at 8am, so Clark invited me to get a cup of tea

But when we got to the canteen to get a cup of tea, it was out of order!

So I said to him, never mind, in Thorpe Park, we can get a burger!

After Thorpe Park, my dad was outside of school, waiting for me
At home, my family had a huge surprise for me
We all celebrated my birthday and Dad gave me a new phone!
Today was one of the greatest days of my life.

Charlie Pablo (14)
Woodside High School, Wood Green

My Winooze That's Unreal

Never again will I remember
The time I ran like a zebra
I ran dizida fast to get away
From the monsters that lay
Lay looden under where I stay.

Latta, it was here,
Here in my boggagly mind
Here in my hoppler
Here in every dream and winooze.

Little do you know
My qwerty little brother
Was under a spell
The lionana.

It was a winooze
My parents were condoozed
It was me
The whole time
Me!

Don't read
The spell is on you too!

Sophia Andi Neofetou (14)
Woodside High School, Wood Green

I Want To Be...

I want to be shizzo, not lenoova,
To try not to be gloomzo or cazoova,
I know a lot of people, who are bronea,
But I aspire to be mayoneeta,
To have a skizzle attitude,
Not to be very ehlude,
To be a pinch of munsun,
A dash of reeton,
With a side of gunter,
Then to mix it all together,
And I will then be the person I want to be.

Elena Rosetta Di Natale (14)
Woodside High School, Wood Green

Young Writers Information

We hope you have enjoyed reading this book - and that you will continue to enjoy it in the coming years.

If you like reading and writing poetry drop us a line, or give us a call, and we'll send you a free information pack.

Alternatively if you would like to order further copies of this book or any of our other titles, then please give us a call or log onto our website at www.youngwriters.co.uk

Young Writers Information
Remus House
Coltsfoot Drive
Peterborough
PE2 9BF
(01733) 890066